I0821674

Digital Footprints

Jeff McHugh and
John Willis

DIGITAL CITIZENSHIP

LIGHTBOX
openlightbox.com

Go to **www.openlightbox.com** and enter this book's unique code.

ACCESS CODE

LBXP8477

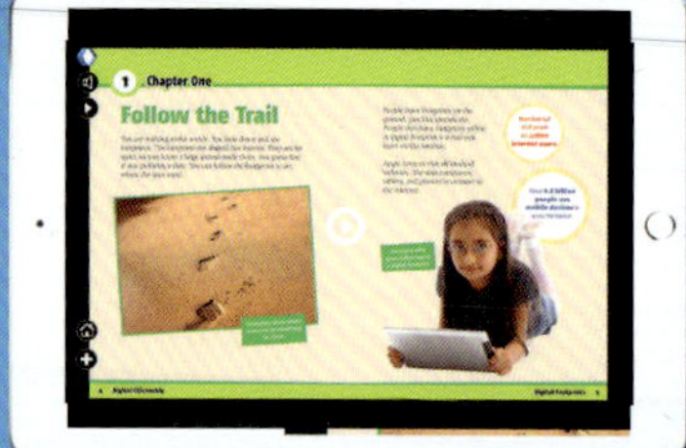

Lightbox is an all-inclusive digital solution for the teaching and learning of curriculum topics in an original, groundbreaking way. Lightbox is based on National Curriculum Standards.

LIGHTBOX SUPPLEMENTARY RESOURCES

SHARE
Share titles within your Learning Management System (LMS) or Library Circulation System

CURRICULUM
Find national and state curriculum correlations

CITATION
Create bibliographical references following the Chicago Manual of Style

STANDARD FEATURES OF LIGHTBOX

AUDIO High-quality narration using text-to-speech system

ACTIVITIES Printable PDFs that can be emailed and graded

SLIDESHOWS Pictorial overviews of key concepts

VIDEOS Embedded high-definition video clips

WEBLINKS Curated links to external, child-safe resources

TRANSPARENCIES Step-by-step layering of maps, diagrams, charts, and timelines

INTERACTIVE MAPS Interactive maps and aerial satellite imagery

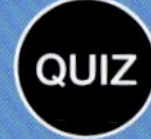

QUIZZES Ten multiple-choice questions that are automatically graded and emailed for teacher assessment

KEY WORDS Matching key concepts to their definitions

This title is part of our Lightbox digital subscription

Lightbox Grades 3–5 Subscription
ISBN 978-1-5105-5424-5

Access hundreds of Lightbox titles with our digital subscription. Sign up for a **FREE** subscription trial at **www.openlightbox.com/trial**

Digital Footprints

Contents

1 Chapter One

Follow the Trail

You are walking in the woods. You look down and see footprints. The footprints are shaped like hooves. They are far apart, so you know a large animal made them. You guess that it was probably a deer. You can follow the footprints to see where the deer went.

Footprints can be used to show where someone or something has been.

People leave footprints on the ground, just like animals do. People also leave footprints online. A digital footprint is a trail you leave on the internet.

Angie loves to visit all kinds of websites. She uses computers, tablets, and phones to connect to the internet.

More than half of all people are **active internet users**.

About **4.3 billion people use mobile devices** to access the internet.

Any device that can go online will leave a digital footprint.

Everyone should be mindful of their digital footprint, especially when using devices owned by someone else.

Anytime Angie uses the internet, she leaves a trail. The things she **posts** online can affect the way people think about her. The sites she visits tell people what she is doing when she is online. Angie tries to leave a trail that shows her good qualities. This is called a positive digital footprint. Angie's digital footprint will be with her forever, so she wants it to show her best traits.

Try This

You can follow your own trail by searching your **browser** history. A browser allows you to visit websites on the internet. Some popular browsers are Microsoft Edge, Google Chrome, and Safari.

Open a browser and visit five different websites. Next, find a button or menu titled "History" at the top of your screen. Click on it to see a list of the sites you just visited. You can click on a site in this list to visit it again. What do the sites in your history say about you? What would you think about someone else if you saw these sites in his or her history?

History of Internet Usage

1989
The World Wide Web is created.

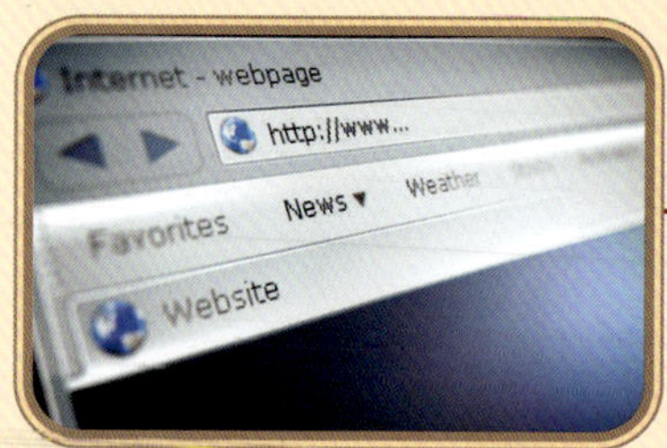

1995
About 16 million people around the world are internet users.

2000
Nearly half of Americans are using the internet to find information.

2004
Facebook, now one of the largest social media sites, is launched.

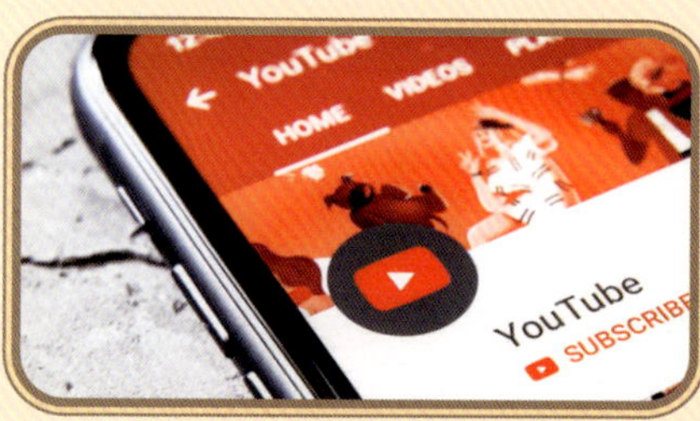

2005
The video sharing platform YouTube is made available to the public.

2016
More than 75 percent of Americans use the internet regularly.

2020
About 3.8 billion people regularly use social media.

Mapping Internet Usage

San Francisco, California, 2007

Twitter, Inc. is created. Its headquarters are in San Francisco. Today, this microblogging service is often used as a major news source.

Beijing, China, 2021

The China Internet Network Information Center (CNNIC) announces that the nation has nearly 1 billion internet users, more than any other country.

2 Chapter Two

Parts of a Digital Footprint

Each digital footprint is **unique**. How? Find out by learning how a digital footprint is made.

A digital footprint has two parts. One part is the trail of websites you visit. Your browser remembers the sites you visit. Many sites record your visit, too. Some even remember the sites you visit before and after them. Angie watches ballet videos online. Her teacher prefers sites about ancient China. Angie's sister likes sites with football information. Each person leaves a different trail of websites.

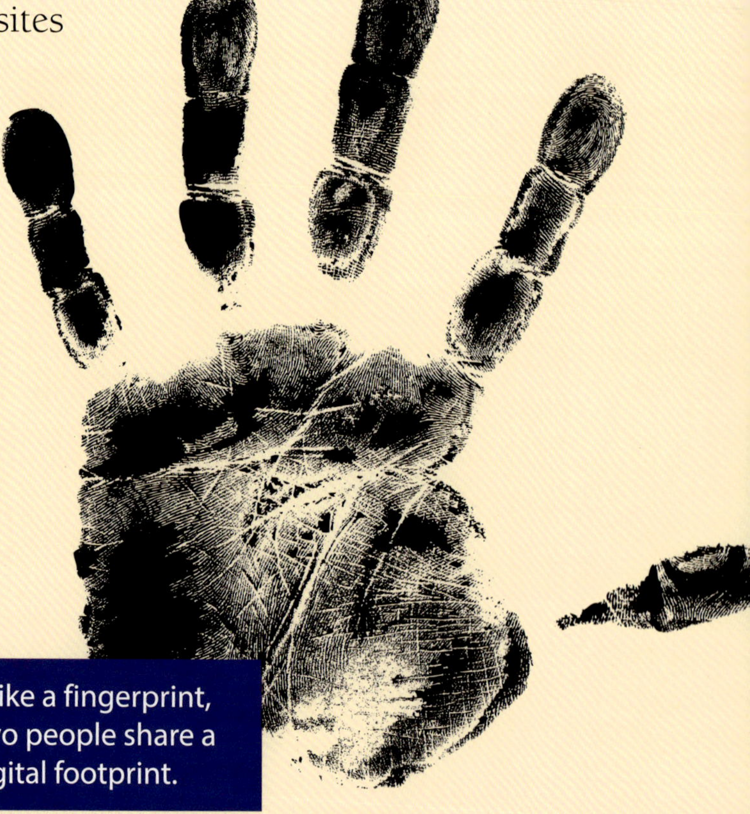

Just like a fingerprint, no two people share a digital footprint.

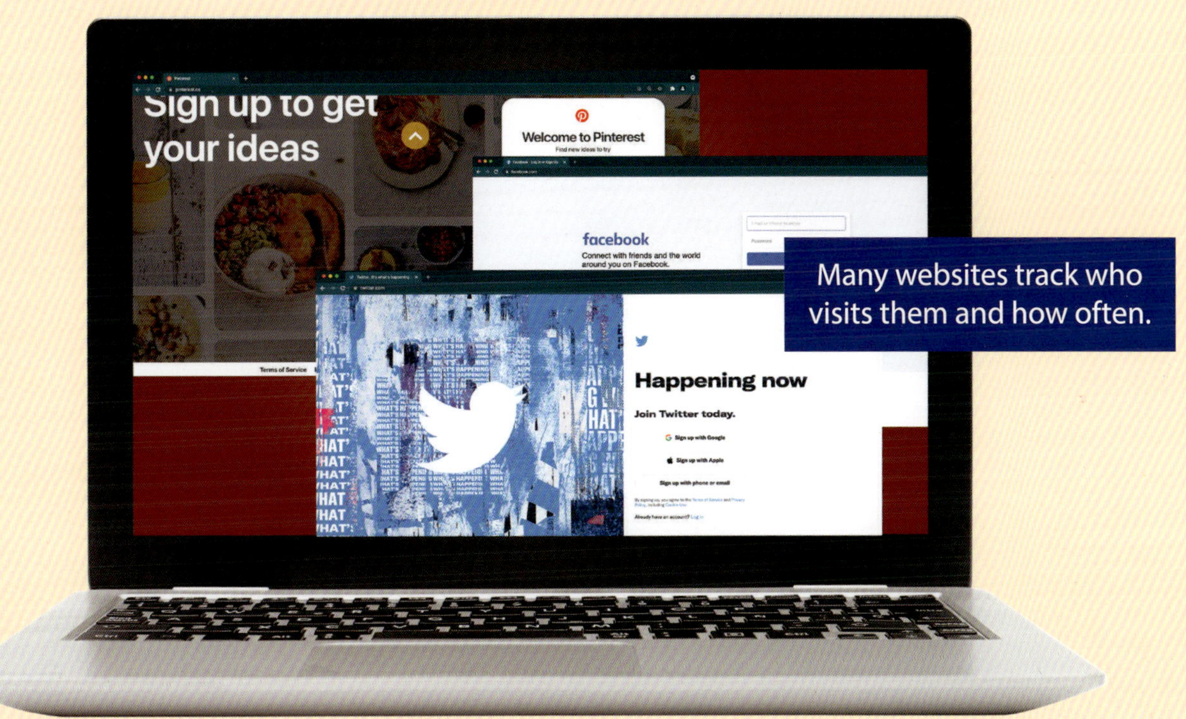

Many websites track who visits them and how often.

Your digital footprint is also made up of the things you share online. There are many ways to share information on the internet. Angie's favorite activity is writing a blog. Sometimes, she includes photos or videos. Angie's dad likes to write comments to people on social media such as Facebook and Twitter. Her friend Kris spends most of his time creating his own website.

Digital footprints are permanent. Once you add something to the internet, it is very difficult to remove it. Closing a page or deleting a post does not mean that it is gone forever. Many sites **archive** everything that people post on them. This means that it still exists somewhere online. People could find it many years in the future. Does that mean you should not share on the internet? Of course not. The internet is a terrific way to share and connect with others. You just need to be smart about sharing.

Be careful which photos you share online. You may not be able to control which people will see them.

Try This

You have learned that the websites you visit become part of your digital footprint. Now take a look at the other part: the information you share on websites.

1. Make a chart with three columns. Write "Text" at the top of the first column. This column is for ideas you shared on blogs, comments you made on websites, and things you wrote on social media sites. Write "Photos" at the top of the second column. Write "Videos" at the top of the third column.
2. Search back through your posts on social media, blogs, and other sites. Try to find things that you have shared on the internet from school or home. Add them to your chart.

Which format—text, photos, or videos—did you share most frequently? Which items are positive additions to your digital footprint?

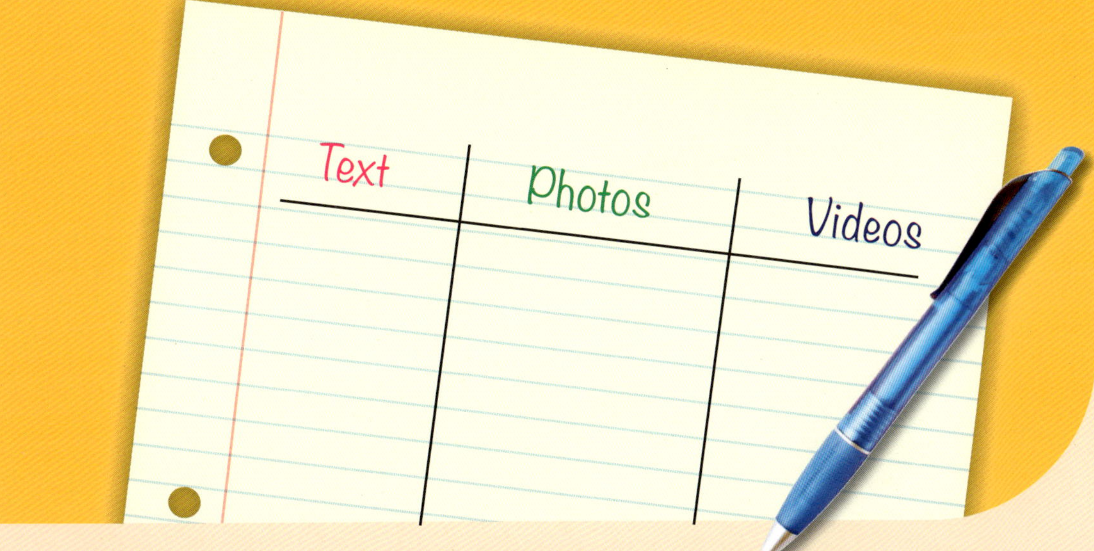

3 Chapter Three

Think Before You Share

Angie thinks of the internet as a tool to share things with a large audience. She creates a positive digital footprint by making good choices about what she shares. This includes any messages, photos, or videos she posts to websites.

Angie always thinks carefully before posting something. People sometimes copy her posts and send them to others. Angie loves the idea of many people reading her posts. However, it also makes her nervous because strangers could see her photos or read her words. She does not want posts that show a bad side of her to spread around the internet.

You cannot always control what happens to the words or photos you post.

Think of how to represent yourself online in the most positive way before posting anything.

Angie follows two simple rules before posting:

1. Respect yourself

You should only post messages, photos, and videos that show something positive about you. Something that seems funny now might be embarrassing later. Before you post, ask yourself these questions:

- What does this post say about me?
- Does it reveal too much about me?
- Is this something I want to share with everyone, including strangers?
- What would my parents or teachers think if they saw this post?

2. Respect others

Sometimes, your posts may involve other people. You might write about a family member on your blog. Maybe you post a photo or video of your friends. You might even comment on another person's post. Make sure you are respectful when posting about others. Ask yourself:

- Would I say this to the person's face?
- How would this post make the person feel if he or she saw it?
- Could someone get the wrong idea about this post?

Be careful about posting things other people might not want shared. Always ask for permission first if you are unsure.

Try This

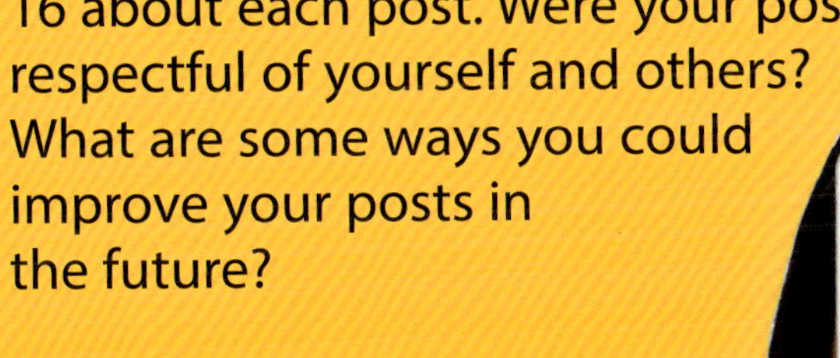

Look back at the list of posts you made in the activity on page 13. Ask the questions listed on pages 15 and 16 about each post. Were your posts respectful of yourself and others? What are some ways you could improve your posts in the future?

4 Chapter Four

Protect Your Privacy

The internet is a great place for sharing, but you need to be careful not to let strangers know too much about you. You should always keep your personal information private online. Your digital footprint can reveal a lot of information about your life. Strangers could use it to learn about you. Do not share your full name, address, or phone number on the internet. You should also keep other personal information, such as your birthday and your school's name, private.

People who steal your information may use it to pretend to be you online.

A username can help people show their interests, such as music, without revealing any personal information.

Many websites ask you to choose a **username** before you can post. A username identifies you to others who visit the site. Your username should be a word or phrase that does not include your name, birthday, or other personal information. Use favorite activities or interests instead. Angie loves dancing ballet. She chose "balletstar" as her username. Angie's sister is a big sports fan. She made her username "bearsfan."

A strong password should include a mixture of letters, symbols, and numbers.

Do not share your usernames and passwords with others. Another person might use your information to log in and pretend to be you. Anything that person posts while logged in as you will affect your digital footprint. By keeping your usernames and passwords private, you control your digital footprint.

Digital footprints can be helpful or harmful. Remember, you are in control of the things you do online. When you use the internet, protect your privacy and make good choices about what you post. Follow these tips and you will leave a positive digital footprint.

Try This

Choosing a username can be fun. Follow these steps to invent some great (and safe) usernames!

1. Draw a line down the middle of a sheet of paper.
2. On the left side of the page, write down some words that describe you. You might choose words such as musical, funny, smart, or sporty.
3. On the right side, write down a list of favorites. Include your favorite hobbies, sports teams, animals, and foods.
4. Match a word from the left with a word from the right to create a unique username, such as "funnytiger." Or add words to your favorites to make "pizzafan" or "fashionstar."

Remember, usernames become part of your digital footprint, so avoid ones that are too silly. The username "stinkymonkey" might seem funny to your friends. However, it may not give others a positive view of you.

funny
musical
smart
sporty

biking
hockey
tiger
pizza

Quiz

1
What does a username do?

2
When was Twitter, Inc. created?

3
What do many websites track?

4
What tool allows you to visit websites on the internet?

5
How many people are active internet users?

6
What two rules should be followed before posting something online?

7
What computer network was created in 1989?

8
What is a digital footprint?

9
What do many sites do with the content posted on them?

10
How many people used social media in 2020?

Answers: 1. Identifies you to others who visit a site **2.** 2007 **3.** Who visits them and how often **4.** A browser **5.** More than half **6.** Respect yourself and respect others **7.** The World Wide Web **8.** A trail you leave on the internet **9.** Archive it **10.** About 3.8 billion

Key Words

archive: to store computer files in a permanent collection

browser: a computer program that lets you find and look through web pages and other parts of the internet

posts: adds words, photos, videos, or other information to the internet

unique: unlike anything else

username: a name that you use to identify yourself on a computer, network, or website

Index

SUPPLEMENTARY RESOURCES

Click on the plus icon ⊕ found in the bottom left corner of each spread to open additional teacher resources.

- Download and print the book's quizzes and activities
- Access curriculum correlations
- Explore additional web applications that enhance the Lightbox experience

LIGHTBOX DIGITAL TITLES

Packed full of integrated media

VIDEOS

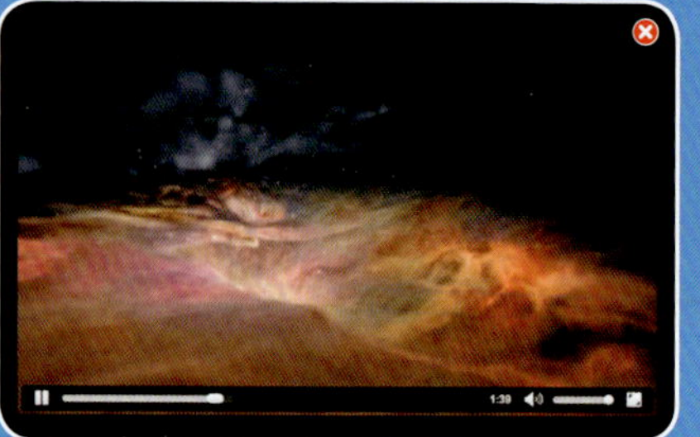

INTERACTIVE MAPS

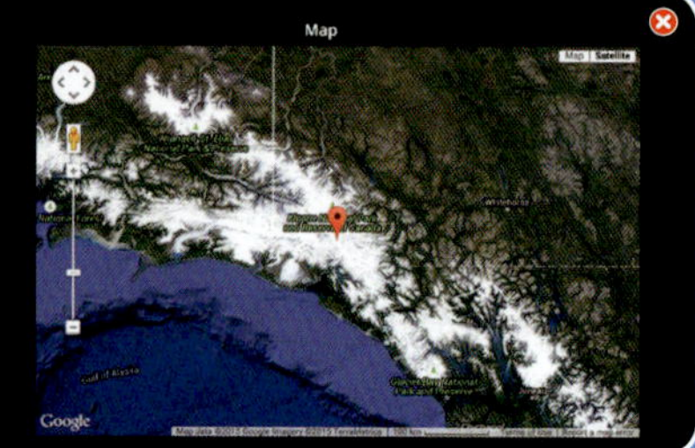

WEBLINKS

SLIDESHOWS

QUIZZES

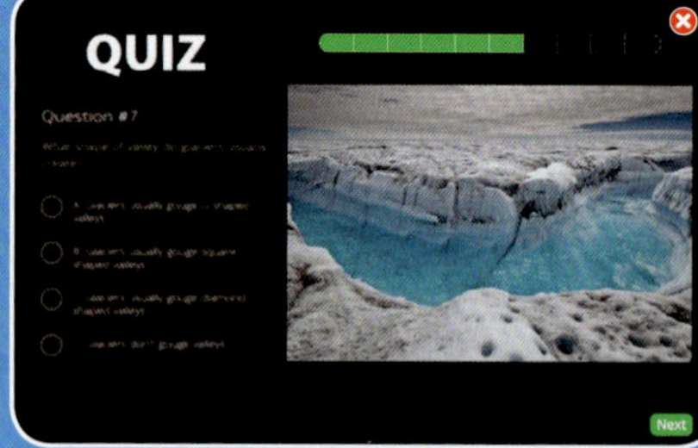

OPTIMIZED FOR

- ✓ TABLETS
- ✓ WHITEBOARDS
- ✓ COMPUTERS
- ✓ AND MUCH MORE!

Published by Lightbox Learning
276 5th Avenue
Suite 704 #917
New York, NY 10001
Website: www.openlightbox.com

First published by Cherry Lake Publishing in 2015

Library of Congress Control Number: 2021939469

ISBN 978-1-5105-5572-3 (hardcover)
ISBN 978-1-5105-5573-0 (multi-user eBook)

Printed in Guangzhou, China
1 2 3 4 5 6 7 8 9 0 25 24 23 22 21

082021
111020

Project Coordinator John Willis
Designer Jean Faye Marie Rodriguez

Photo Credits
Every reasonable effort has been made to trace ownership and to obtain permission to reprint copyright material. The publisher would be pleased to have any errors or omissions brought to its attention so that they may be corrected in subsequent printings.

The publisher acknowledges Getty Images as its primary image supplier for this title.